SO-ADW-753

ANDREW FULLER

Other Books by John Piper

ANDREW FULLER

Holy Faith, Worthy Gospel, World Mission

JOHN PIPER

Foreword by Michael A. G. Haykin

CROSSWAY®

WHEATON, ILLINOIS

Andrew Fuller: Holy Faith, Worthy Gospel, World Mission

Copyright © 2016 by Desiring God Foundation

Published by Crossway
   1300 Crescent Street
   Wheaton, Illinois 60187

All rights reserved. No part of this publication may be reproduced, stored in a retrieval system, or transmitted in any form by any means, electronic, mechanical, photocopy, recording, or otherwise, without the prior permission of the publisher, except as provided for by USA copyright law. Crossway® is a registered trademark in the United States of America.

Cover design: Josh Dennis

Cover image: Glenn Harrington

First printing 2016

Printed in the United States of America

Scripture quotations are from the ESV® Bible (The Holy Bible, English Standard Version®), copyright © 2001 by Crossway, a publishing ministry of Good News Publishers. Used by permission. All rights reserved.

All emphases in Scripture quotations have been added by the author.

Trade paperback ISBN: 978-1-4335-5189-5
ePub ISBN: 978-1-4335-5192-5
PDF ISBN: 978-1-4335-5190-1
Mobipocket ISBN: 978-1-4335-5191-8

Library of Congress Cataloging-in-Publication Data

Names: Piper, John, 1946– author.
Title: Andrew Fuller : holy faith, worthy gospel, world mission / John Piper.
Description: Wheaton: Crossway, 2016. | Includes bibliographical references.
Identifiers: LCCN 2016000996 (print) | LCCN 2016013575 (ebook) | ISBN 9781433551895 (tp) | ISBN 9781433551925 (epub) | ISBN 9781433551901 (pdf) | ISBN 9781433551918 (mobi)
Subjects: LCSH: Fuller, Andrew, 1754–1815. | Baptists—England—Clergy—Biography.
Classification: LCC BX6495.F75 P57 2016 (print) | LCC BX6495.F75 (ebook) | DDC 286/.1092—dc23
LC record available at http://lccn.loc.gov/2016000996

Crossway is a publishing ministry of Good News Publishers.

VP		26	25	24	23	22	21	20	19	18	17	16
15	14	13	12	11	10	9	8	7	6	5	4	3	2	1

Contents

Foreword

Near the beginning of the funeral sermon that John Ryland Jr. (1753–1825) preached for Andrew Fuller in 1815,
Ryland described Fuller as "perhaps the most judicious
and able theological writer that ever belonged to our [i.e.,
the Calvinistic Baptist] denomination."[1] Although Fuller
was Ryland's closest friend and confidant, Ryland's judg-
ment is by no means skewed. Joseph Belcher, the editor
of the standard nineteenth-century edition of Fuller's collected works, believed that those works would "go down
to posterity side by side with the immortal works of the
elder president Edwards [i.e., Jonathan Edwards Sr.],"[2]
while Charles Haddon Spurgeon described Fuller as "the
greatest theologian" of his century.[3] And in an allusion to

1. John Ryland Jr., *The Indwelling and Righteousness of Christ No Security against
Corporeal Death, but the Source of Spiritual and Eternal Life* (London: W. Button & Son,
1815), 2–3. Ryland went on to write the classic study of Fuller's life: *The Work of Faith,
the Labour of Love, and the Patience of Hope, Illustrated; in the Life and Death of the
Reverend Andrew Fuller* (London: W. Button & Son, 1816). The same publisher published
a second edition of this biography in 1818.

2. "Preface to the Complete American Edition," in *The Complete Works of the Rev.
Andrew Fuller*, ed. Joseph Belcher, 3 vols. (1845; repr., Harrisonburg, VA: Sprinkle,
1988), 1:viii.

3. Quoted in Gilbert Laws, *Andrew Fuller: Pastor, Theologian, Ropeholder* (London:
Carey, 1942), 127.

his weighty theological influence, the nineteenth-century Welsh author David Phillips called Fuller the "elephant of Kettering."[4]

Despite these glowing tributes to Fuller as a theologian, come the twentieth century, he was largely forgotten. There were only two biographies of him during this entire period, those of Gilbert Laws and Arthur H. Kirkby. Neither was a major study, and Kirkby's was but a booklet.[5] With the advent of the present century, however, there has been a veritable renaissance of scholarly and popular interest in Fuller and his theological perspectives.[6] And in this renaissance, this essay by Dr. John Piper provides those interested in Fuller with a unique perspective. A New Testament scholar by training, Piper has devoted the bulk of his ministry to the regular exposition of the Scriptures in the context of the local church. He has an abiding interest in church history, having been exposed, at an early stage in his walk with God, to the riches of the writings of Jonathan Edwards, who also deeply shaped Fuller, and those of C. S. Lewis. And for many years, at the annual midwinter Desiring God Conference for pastors, Piper would give a paper dealing with a major figure from church history.[7] I was fascinated to learn that in 2007

4. David Phillips, *Memoir of the Life, Labors, and Extensive Usefulness of the Rev. Christmas Evans* (New York: M. W. Dodd, 1843), 74.

5. Laws, *Andrew Fuller*; Arthur H. Kirkby, *Andrew Fuller (1754–1815)* (London: Independent, 1961).

6. For an overview of this resurgence of interest, see Nathan A. Finn, "The Renaissance in Andrew Fuller Studies: A Bibliographic Essay," *The Southern Baptist Journal of Theology* 17, no. 2 (Summer 2013): 44–61.

7. Many of these have been published in Crossway's series The Swans Are Not Silent.

he had decided to speak on Fuller. And as the following study reveals, Piper clearly regards Fuller as having been a significant "game changer" in the history of God's people. As Piper stresses, one key area of Fuller's great impact is the globalization of Christianity: Fuller provides the pioneers of the modern missionary movement with a robust theology of missions that was hammered out in the context of theological controversy with hyper-Calvinism and Sandemanianism.

While Fuller excelled as an apologist, he was also a gifted expositor of Scripture and even wrote a biographical memoir of his close friend Samuel Pearce of Birmingham, who died in 1799 at the age of thirty-three. Modeled after Jonathan Edwards's life of David Brainerd, this memoir recounted the life of one whom Fuller regarded as a sterling model of evangelical and mission-minded piety. Through the medium of Fuller's book, Pearce's extraordinary passion for Christ—which led to his being labeled the "seraphic Pearce" by contemporaries—and his zeal for missions had a powerful impact on his generation, nearly as much as Fuller's formal treatises on missions. One London diarist noted in 1805 that he had been reading Fuller's memoir of Pearce, "that truly eminent and pious man." It led the writer to cry out, "Oh that I had but a double portion of his spirit, that I may be as useful, as zealous, as active, as diligent, as pious, as affectionate, as worthy of imitation, as fit for glory as he was!" May this be the reaction of the reader of this little book on Fuller. May it not only inform the mind, but also enflame the heart![8]

Michael A. G. Haykin,

Professor of Church History and Biblical Spirituality,

The Southern Baptist Theological Seminary;

Director, The Andrew Fuller Center for Baptist Studies

---

8. For more recent studies, see Laws, *Andrew Fuller*; Kirkby, *Andrew Fuller (1754–1815)*; and Phil Roberts, "Andrew Fuller," in Timothy George and David S. Dockery, eds., *Baptist Theologians* (Nashville: Broadman, 1990), 121–39. See also two very fine unpublished theses on Fuller: Doyle L. Young, "The Place of Andrew Fuller in the Developing Modern Missions Movement" (PhD diss., Southwestern Baptist Theological Seminary, 1981); Thomas Kennedy Ascol, "The Doctrine of Grace: A Critical Analysis of Federalism in the Theologies of John Gill and Andrew Fuller" (PhD diss., Southwestern Baptist Theological Seminary, 1989). Also see the excellent study by E. F. Clipsham, "Andrew Fuller and Fullerism: A Study in Evangelical Calvinism," *The Baptist Quarterly* 20 (1963–1964): 99–114, 146–54, 214–25, 268–76.

An Andrew Fuller Chronology

Compiled by Ian Hugh Clary

1754   February 6: born in Wicken, Cambridgeshire

Jonathan Edwards's *Freedom of the Will* published

1761   Moved to Soham with family

1769   November: Conversion

1770   Baptized

Joined Particular Baptist church in Soham, pastored by John Eve (d. 1782)

1775   May 3: Ordained pastor of church in Soham

1776   Married Sarah Gardiner of Burwell, Cambridgeshire

1782   October: Moved to Kettering to pastor the Particular Baptist church

1784   June: Northamptonshire Association issued the "Call to Prayer"

1785   *The Gospel Worthy of All Acceptation* published

1792   August 23: Wife Sarah died

October: Particular Baptist Society for Propagating of the Gospel among the Heathen formed, later to be called the Baptist Missionary Society; Fuller appointed as its first secretary

1793   *The Calvinistic and Socinian Systems Examined and Compared as to Their Moral Tendency* published

       June: William Carey, his family, and John Thomas sent to India by the Baptist Missionary Society

1794   December 30: Married Ann Coles of Ampthill, Bedfordshire

1798   Awarded an honorary Doctor of Divinity from Princeton

1799   *The Gospel Its Own Witness* published

       The first of five fund-raising trips to Scotland

1805   Awarded an honorary Doctor of Divinity from Yale

1810   *Strictures on Sandemanianism* published

1811   John Keen Hall appointed as Fuller's assistant

1815   May 7: Died in Kettering

Chapter One

A Mind for Modern Missions

Andrew Fuller's impact on history, by the time Jesus returns, may very well be far greater and different than it is now. My assessment at this point is that his primary impact on history has been the impetus that his life and thought gave to modern missions, specifically through the Baptist Missionary Society's sending of William Carey to India in 1793 with the support of Fuller, the society's first secretary. That historical moment—the sending of William Carey and his team—marked the opening of the modern missionary movement.

The Unleashing of Modern Missions

William Carey was the morning star of modern missions. Between 1793 and 1865, a missionary movement never before seen in the history of the world reached virtually all the coastlands on earth. Then, in 1865, Hudson Taylor founded the China Inland Mission, and from 1865 until

1934, another wave of missionary activity was released so that by 1974 virtually all the inlands—all the geographic countries of the world—were reached with the gospel. In 1934, Cameron Townsend founded Wycliffe Bible Translators, which focused not on geographic areas or political states but on people groups with distinct languages and dialects and cultures—and gradually the church awakened, especially at the Lausanne Congress in 1974, to the biblical reality of "every tribe and language and people and nation" (Rev. 5:9; cf. 7:9)—and the missionary focus of the church shifted from unreached *geography* to the unreached *peoples* of the world.

We are in the midst of this third era of modern missions. Today the great reality, as documented in Philip Jenkins's *The Next Christendom*,[1] is that the center of gravity in missions is moving away from Europe and the United States to the South and East. Places we once considered mission fields are now centers of Christian influence and are major missionary-sending forces in the world.[2]

Andrew Fuller's Impact

You won't read it in the secular history books or hear it on the nightly news, but judged by almost any standard, this

---

1. Philip Jenkins, *The Next Christendom: The Coming of Global Christianity*, 3rd ed. (New York: Oxford University Press, 2011). See also Jenkins, *The New Faces of Christianity: Believing the Bible in the Global South* (New York: Oxford University Press, 2006).

2. Andrew Walls would view it a little differently than Jenkins: "While some scholars such as Philip Jenkins emphasize a shift of power from Western churches to those south of the equator, Walls sees instead a new polycentrism: the riches of a hundred places learning from each other." Tim Stafford, "Historian Ahead of His Time," *Christianity Today* 51, no. 2 (February 2007): 89.

modern missionary movement—the spread of the Christian faith to every country and almost all the peoples of the world—is the most important historical development in the last two hundred years. Stephen Neill, in the conclusion to his *History of Christian Missions*, wrote,

> The cool and rational eighteenth century [which ended with William Carey's departure for India] was hardly a promising seedbed for Christian growth; but out of it came a greater outburst of Christian missionary enterprise than had been seen in all the centuries before.[3]

So how did it come about that the "cool and rational" eighteenth century gave birth to the greatest missionary movement in world history—a movement that continues to this day, which, if you're willing, *you* can be a part of? God's ways are higher than our ways, and his judgments are unfathomable and inscrutable (Rom. 11:33). More factors led to this great movement than any human can know. All I want to do is document one of them—just one of ten thousand things God did to unleash this great Christ-exalting, gospel-advancing, church-expanding, evil-confronting, Satan-conquering, culture-transforming, soul-saving, hell-robbing, Christian-refreshing, truth-intensifying missionary movement.[4]

---

3. Stephen Neill, *A History of Christian Missions* (New York: Penguin, 1964), 571.

4. I use the terms *Christian-refreshing* and *truth-intensifying* because in Andrew Fuller's life, there is a reciprocal relationship between spiritual life and biblical truth, on the one hand, and missions, on the other hand. In one direction, spiritual life and biblical truth give rise to missions. And in the other direction, engagement in the missionary enterprise awakens and sustains new levels of spiritual life and sharpens and deepens and intensifies our grasp of biblical truth. I will focus on the first, but here are some glimpses into the effect missions had on Fuller's life. On July 18, 1794, he wrote in his diary:

The reason I wrote at the beginning of this chapter that it is totally possible that Andrew Fuller's impact on history, by the time Jesus returns, will be far greater and different than it is now, is that three volumes of his writings are still in print, and he was an unusually brilliant theologian. So, quite apart from his influence on the rise of modern missions, his biblical insights may have an impact for good on future generations all out of proportion to his obscure place in the small town of Kettering, England. We will see some of his theological genius as we work our way backward from effect to cause—from his engagement with the new missionary movement to the spiritual life and theology that set it in motion.

Within the last year or two, we have formed a missionary society; and have been enabled to send out two of our brethren to the East Indies. My heart has been greatly interested in this work. Surely I never felt more genuine love to God and to his cause in my life. I bless God that this work has been a means of reviving my soul. If nothing else comes of it, I and many others have obtained a spiritual advantage. (quoted in Peter Morden, *Offering Christ to the World: Andrew Fuller (1754–1815) and the Revival of Eighteenth Century Particular Baptist Life*, Studies in Baptist History and Thought 8 [Carlisle: Paternoster, 2003], 167)

Six months earlier he had written to John Ryland:

I have found the more I do for Christ, the better it is with me. I never enjoyed so much the pleasures of religion, as I have within the last two years, since we have engaged in the Mission business. Mr. Whitfield [*sic*] used to say, "the more a man does for God, the more he may." (quoted in Morden, *Offering Christ*, 167)

In one direction, when your love for Christ is enflamed and your grasp of the gospel is clear, a passion for world missions follows. In the other direction, when you are involved in missions—when you are laying down your life to rescue people from perishing—it tends to authenticate your faith, and deepen your assurance, and sweeten your fellowship with Jesus, and heighten your love for people, and sharpen your doctrines of Christ and heaven and hell. In other words, spiritual life and right doctrine are good for missions, and missions is good for spiritual life and right doctrine.

Baptist church in Kettering, Northamptonshire, where
Fuller preached and pastored from 1782 to 1815

Chapter Two

Great Gain, Great Loss, Great Perseverance

Andrew Fuller died on May 7, 1815, at the age of sixty-one. He had been the pastor of the Baptist church in Kettering (population, about three thousand) for thirty-two years. Before that, he was the pastor at Soham, and before that, he was a boy growing up on his parents' farm and getting a simple education. He had no formal theological training but became the leading theological spokesman for the Particular Baptists[1] in his day. He began to do occasional preaching in his home church of Soham at age seventeen, and when he was twenty-one, they called him to be the pastor.

The year after he became the pastor at Soham, he married Sarah Gardiner. (It was 1776—the year America declared

---

1. The term *Particular Baptist* is a technical term taken from the phrase *particular redemption*, one of the tenets of the Calvinistic Baptists. Therefore, *Particular* Baptists were the Calvinistic Baptists, in distinction from the *General* (or Arminian) Baptists.

independence from Britain.) In the sixteen years before she died, the couple had eleven children, of whom eight died in infancy or early childhood. Sarah died two months before the Baptist Missionary Society was formed in October 1792.

It is often this way in the ministry: the greatest gain and the greatest loss within two months. "Whoever loses his life for my sake will find it" (Matt. 10:39). "Unless a grain of wheat falls into the earth and dies, it remains alone; but if it dies, it bears much fruit" (John 12:24). Fuller did marry again. In 1794 he married Ann Coles, who outlived him by ten years.

An Overwhelmed Life

During these forty years of pastoral ministry in Soham and Kettering, Fuller tried to do more than one man can do well. He tried to raise a family, pastor a church, engage the destructive doctrinal errors of his day with endless writing, and function as the leader of the Baptist Missionary Society, which he and a band of brothers had founded. He regularly felt overwhelmed. In 1801, he wrote in a letter:

> [Samuel] Pearce's memoirs are now loudly called for [that is, people were calling for him to write the memoirs of his friend, which he did]. I sit down almost in despair. . . . My wife looks at me with a tear ready to drop, and says, "My dear, you have hardly time to speak to me." My friends at home are kind, but they also say, "You have no time to see us or know us and you will soon be worn out." Amidst all this there is

"Come again to Scotland—come to Portsmouth—come to Plymouth—come to Bristol."[2]

It was a little band of Baptist pastors, including William Carey, who had formed the Baptist Missionary Society on October 2, 1792. Fuller, more than anyone else, felt the burden of what it meant that William Carey and John Thomas (and later, others) left everything for India in dependence, under God, on this band of brothers. One of them, John Ryland, recorded the story from which came the famous "rope holder" image. He wrote that Carey said:

> Our undertaking to India really appeared to me, on its commencement, to be somewhat like a few men, who were deliberating about the importance of penetrating into a deep mine, which had never before been explored, [and] we had no one to guide us; and while we were thus deliberating, Carey, as it were, said "Well, I will go down, if you will hold the rope." But before he went down . . . he, as it seemed to me, took an oath from each of us, at the mouth of the pit, to this effect—that "while we lived, we should never let go of the rope."[3]

Fuller served as the main promoter, thinker, fund-raiser, and letter writer of the society for over twenty-one years. He held that rope more firmly and with greater conscientiousness than anyone else. When he said, above, that in all his

---

2. Peter Morden, *Offering Christ to the World: Andrew Fuller (1754–1815) and the Revival of Eighteenth Century Particular Baptist Life*, Studies in Baptist History and Thought 8 (Carlisle: Paternoster, 2003), 153–54.

3. Ibid., 136.

William Carey (1761–1834)

pastoral labors he heard "Come again to Scotland—come to Portsmouth—come to Plymouth—come to Bristol," he meant that churches were calling him to come and represent the mission. So he traveled, continuously speaking to raise support for the mission. He wrote the regular *Periodical Accounts*. He supplied news to the *Baptist Annual Register*, the *Evangelical Magazine*, and the *Baptist Magazine*. He took the lead role in selecting new missionaries. He wrote regularly to the missionaries on the field and to people at home.[4]

4. See ibid., 136–37, for a fuller account of his engagements.

Tireless Pastoral Labors

Fuller did all this while knowing his pastoral work was suffering. He did not have an assistant at Kettering until 1811 (John Hall), four years before he died. In October 1794, he lamented in a letter to Ryland how the mission work was compromising the church work: "I long to visit my congregation that I may know of their spiritual concerns and preach to their cases."[5] The love he felt for his people is expressed in a letter he wrote to a wayward member that he was pursuing:

> When a parent loses . . . a child nothing but the recovery of that child can heal the wound. If he could have many other children, that would not do it. . . . Thus it is with me towards you. Nothing but your return to God and the Church can heal the wound.[6]

Fuller pressed on, faithfully feeding his flock with faithful expository preaching.

> Beginning April 1790, he expounded successively Psalms, Isaiah, Joel, Amos, Hosea, Micah, Nahum, Habakkuk, Zephaniah, Jeremiah, Lamentations, Daniel, Haggai, Zechariah, Malachi, Genesis, Matthew, Luke, John, Revelation, Acts, Romans, and First Corinthians as far as 4:5.[7]

---

5. Ibid., 111.

6. Michael A. G. Haykin, ed. *The Armies of the Lamb: The Spirituality of Andrew Fuller* (Dundas, ON: Joshua, 2001), 36.

7. Tom Nettles, "Preface to the New Edition: Why Andrew Fuller?," in *The Complete Works of the Rev. Andrew Fuller*, ed. Joseph Belcher, 3 vols. (1845; repr., Harrisonburg, VA: Sprinkle, 1988), 1:[unnumbered]. Henceforth, this set will be cited as Fuller, *Works*, with the appropriate volume and page numbers.

The people did not seem to begrudge their pastor's wider ministry for the missionary society. One young deacon entered in his diary two weeks before Fuller's death,

> What a loss as individuals and as a church we are going to sustain. Him that has so long fed us with the bread of life, that has so affectionately, so faithfully, and so fervently counsell'd, exhorted, reproved, and animated; by doctrine, by precept, and by example the people of his charge; him who has liv'd so much for others! Shall we no more hear his voice?[8]

And when he was home from his travels, his life was one form of work or another. His second wife, Ann, once told him that "he allowed himself no time for recreation." Fuller answered, "O no: all my recreation is a change of work."[9] His son Gunton recorded that even in 1815, just a few months before his death, he was still working at his desk "upwards of twelve hours a day."[10]

Extraordinary Suffering

Woven into all this work, making his perseverance all the more astonishing, was the extraordinary suffering, especially his losses. He lost eight children and his first wife. On July 10, 1792, he wrote, "My family afflictions have almost overwhelmed me, and what is yet before me I know not! For about a month past the affliction of my dear compan-

---

8. Morden, *Offering Christ*, 112.
9. Fuller, *Works*, 1:110.
10. Morden, *Offering Christ*, 183.

ion has been extremely heavy." Then on July 25, "Oh my God, my soul is cast down within me! The afflictions of my family seemed too heavy for me. Oh, Lord, I am oppressed, undertake for me!"[11] When his wife died one month later (August 23, 1792), having lost eight of her children, Fuller wrote these lines:

> The tender parent wails no more her loss,
> Nor labors more beneath life's heavy load;
> The anxious soul, released from fears and woes,
> Has found her home, her children, and her God.[12]

---

11. Fuller, *Works*, 1:58–59.
12. Ibid., 1:59–61.

Chapter Three

Andrew Fuller the Thinker

Andrew Fuller's tireless perseverance through many afflictions formed the personal, pastoral, missionary context of his engagement with the spiritual and doctrinal errors of his day. And for all his activism, it is his controversial and doctrinal writing that served the cause of world missions most. Virtually all of Fuller's students agree that he was the most influential theologian of the Particular Baptists. "Fuller," one writes, "was pre-eminently the thinker, and no movement can go far without a thinker."[1]

What I will try to do here and in the following chapters is show how his battle with hyper-Calvinism (or what he more often called *High Calvinism*) recovered and preserved a kind of preaching that is essential for missions, and his battle with Sandemanianism recovered and preserved a

---

1. Peter Morden, *Offering Christ to the World: Andrew Fuller (1754–1815) and the Revival of Eighteenth Century Particular Baptist Life*, Studies in Baptist History and Thought 8 (Carlisle: Paternoster, 2003), 137, citing E. F. Clipsham, who, in turn, was quoting B. Grey Griffith.

kind of vital faith that is essential for missions. And in both cases, the battles were distinctly exegetical and doctrinal, even though the all-important outcomes were deeply experiential and globally practical.

Enlightenment Contemporaries and Particular Baptists

Of course, Andrew Fuller the thinker, the theologian, did not arise in a vacuum. Besides the secular rationalism of David Hume (1711–1776) in Britain and Rousseau (1712–1778) in France and Thomas Paine (1737–1809) in America—all contemporaries of Andrew Fuller—there was the Great Awakening in America and the Evangelical Awakening in Britain. Both George Whitefield (1714–1770) and John Wesley (1703–1791) were in their prime when Fuller was born in 1754.

The Particular Baptists did not like either of these evangelical leaders. Wesley was not a Calvinist, and Whitefield's Calvinism was suspect, to say the least, because of the kind of evangelistic preaching he did. The Particular Baptists spoke derisively of Whitefield's "Arminian dialect."[2] Fuller grew up in what he called a High Calvinistic—or hyper-Calvinistic—church. He said later that the minister at the church in Soham (John Eve) had "little or nothing to say to the unconverted."[3] Fuller's greatest theological achievement was to see and defend and spread the truth that historic, biblical Calvinism fully

---

2. Morden, *Offering Christ*, 20.
3. Ibid., 27.

embraced the offer of the gospel to all people without exception.

Fuller immersed himself in the Scriptures and in the historic tradition flowing from Augustine through Calvin through the Puritans down to Jonathan Edwards. The Bible was always paramount. In Fuller's words, "Lord, thou hast given me a determination to take up no principle at second-hand; but to search for everything at the pure fountain of thy word."[4] That is one of the main reasons why it is so profitable to read Fuller to this very day: he is so freshly biblical.

His Great Mentors

But he is wide open about who his great mentors were. And we should know them. He searched both the Scriptures and the history of doctrine to see if he could find this High Calvinism that had so infected and controlled his denomination—the view that opposed offering the gospel to all men and said it could not be the duty of the unregenerate men to believe on Jesus, and therefore one should not tell them they should do what they have no duty to do. That was the reasoning of hyper-Calvinism.[5] On the basis of his thorough research, Fuller responded:

---

4. Fuller, *Works*, 1:20 (see chap. 2, n. 7).

5. The two most influential authors representing High Calvinism—at least the ones who influenced Particular Baptists most—were John Brine (1703–1765) and John Gill (1697–1771). Morden comments that Timothy George and others have made attempts to rehabilitate Gill and to rebut the charge that he was a hyper-Calvinist, "but attempts to defend him from the charge of high Calvinism are ultimately unconvincing" (*Offering Christ*, 15). Morden offers a quotation illustrating Gill's attitude toward a free offer of the gospel:

Neither Augustine nor Calvin, who each in his day defended predestination, and the other doctrines connected with it, ever appear to have thought of denying it to be the duty of every sinner who has heard the gospel to repent and believe in Jesus Christ. Neither did the other Reformers, nor the Puritans of the sixteenth century, nor the divines at the Synod of Dort, (who opposed Arminius) nor any of the nonconformists of the seventeenth century, so far as I have any acquaintance with their writings, ever so much as hesitate upon this subject.[6]

John Calvin played a relatively minor role in shaping Fuller's thinking directly. Fuller was immersed in the Puritans and quoted more from Charnock, Goodwin, Bunyan, and Owen than from Calvin.[7] In fact, by Fuller's own testimony, John Owen ranked first in his esteem of all the writers that influenced him: "I never met with anything of importance in his writings on which I saw any reason to animadvert; so far from it, *that I know of no writer for whom I have so great an esteem.*"[8]

That there are universal offers of grace and salvation made to all men, I utterly deny; nay I deny that they are made to any; no not to God's elect; grace and salvation are provided for them in the everlasting covenant, procured for them by Christ, published and revealed in the gospel and applied by the Spirit. (John Gill, *Sermons and Tracts* [London, 1778], 3:269–70, quoted in Morden, *Offering Christ*, 14)

Fuller himself certainly saw Gill as a High Calvinist responsible for much of the evangelistic deadness among his fellow Particular Baptists: "I perceived . . . that the system of Bunyan was not the same as [John Gill's]; for while he maintained the doctrines of election and predestination, he nevertheless held with the free offer of salvation to sinners without distinction" (Morden, *Offering Christ*, 31).

6. Fuller, *Works*, 2:367.
7. He quotes from Calvin only once in the first edition of his most influential book, *The Gospel Worthy of All Acceptation*. Morden concludes, "There is no direct link between Calvin's writings and *The Gospel Worthy*" (Morden, *Offering Christ*, 35).
8. Fuller, *Works*, 1:39, emphasis added.

The Influence of Jonathan Edwards

But even if he esteemed Owen above all others, almost everyone who studies Fuller's works agrees that Jonathan Edwards was the most decisively influential in helping him break free from his hyper-Calvinistic roots.[9] Fuller admits that, after the Bible itself, it was Edwards who provided the keys that unlocked the door out of hyper-Calvinist reasoning. We will see that this was true for both the Sandemanian and the hyper-Calvinist controversies.

David Bebbington says that Jonathan Edwards "stands at the headwaters" of eighteenth-century evangelicalism.[10] That is certainly true for Andrew Fuller. To give you a flavor of the way he felt about Edwards, ten days before Fuller died on May 7, 1815, he dictated a letter to John Ryland, one of the band of brothers who founded the mission together with him. The point of the letter was to defend Edwards:

> We have heard some, who have been giving out of late that "if Sutcliff and some others had preached more of Christ and less of Jonathan Edwards, they would have been more useful." If those who talk thus, preached Christ half as much as Jonathan Edwards did, and were half as useful as he was, their usefulness would be double what it is.[11]

---

9. Edwards, most agree, was "probably the most powerful and important extra-biblical influence" on Fuller (Morden, *Offering Christ*, 49).

10. David Bebbington, *Evangelicalism in Modern Britain: A History from the 1730s to the 1980s* (London: Unwin Hyman, 1989), 6.

11. Fuller, *Works*, 1:101.

Jonathan Edwards (1703–1758)

Edwards's *Freedom of the Will*

Fuller was born in 1754, four years before Jonathan Edwards died, and the year Edwards published his hugely influential book *The Freedom of the Will*. I mention Edwards's book on the will because in it Fuller found one of the keys that unlocked the unbiblical prison of hyper-Calvinism.

The hyper-Calvinist reasoning went like this, Fuller summarizes:

It is absurd and cruel to require of any man what is beyond his power to perform; and as the Scriptures declare that "No man can come to Christ, except the Father draw him," and that "The natural man receiveth not the things of the Spirit of God, neither can he know them, because they are spiritually discerned," it is concluded that these are things to which the sinner, while unregenerate, is under no obligation.[12]

"It is a kind of maxim with such persons," Fuller explains, "that 'none can be obliged to act spiritually, but spiritual men.'"[13]

The practical conclusion that hyper-Calvinists drew was that faith in Christ is not a duty for the non-elect. It is not a duty for the unregenerate. Therefore, you never call for faith indiscriminately. You never stand before a group of people—whether in Britain or in India—and say, "Believe on the Lord Jesus Christ!" You never exhort, plead, call, command, urge.

As we will see in chapter 4, Fuller the thinker recognized that such teaching is unfaithful to God's Word. The modern missions movement would grow out of a more biblical understanding of gospel proclamation to the lost.

12. Ibid., 2:376.
13. Ibid., 2:360.

Chapter Four

Fuller against Hyper-Calvinism

One of Fuller's critics, John Martin, pastor at Grafton Street, Westminster, wrote,

> Sinners in my opinion, are more frequently converted, and believers more commonly edified, by a narrative of facts concerning Jesus Christ, and by a clear, connected statement of the doctrines of grace, and blessings of the gospel, than by all the exhortations and expostulations that were ever invented.[1]

But in fact, the hyper-Calvinists were not passionately telling the narrative of the gospel story to the lost and were opposed to the new mission to India. Peter Morden points out that "the prevalence of high Calvinism had led not only to a refusal to 'offer Christ' but also to a general suspicion of all human 'means', such as ministerial training

---

1. Quoted in Peter Morden, *Offering Christ to the World: Andrew Fuller (1754–1815) and the Revival of Eighteenth Century Particular Baptist Life*, Studies in Baptist History and Thought 8 (Carlisle: Paternoster, 2003), 57.

and associating."[2] The effect of this rationalistic distortion of the biblical Calvinism was that the churches were lifeless[3] and the denomination of the Particular Baptists was dying.

Fuller, who knew only High Calvinism in his early ministry, said in 1774, "I . . . durst not, for some years, address an invitation to the unconverted to come to Jesus."[4] He went on to say, "I conceive there is scarcely a minister amongst us whose preaching has not been more or less influenced by the lethargic systems of the age."[5] The price had been huge: in the forty years after 1718, the Particular Baptists declined from 220 congregations to 150.[6]

A "Warrant of Faith"?

If you ask, How then did anyone get saved under this system? the answer was that here and there God would give what High Calvinists called a "warrant of faith." That is, there would be some token granted by the Holy Spirit to signify that the persons were regenerate and elect and therefore had a "warrant" to believe. For example, one way God did this, they believed, was by forcibly suggesting a Scripture to one's mind. This happened to Fuller at age thirteen

---

2. Morden, *Offering Christ*, 45.

3. One example of the emotional fallout of High Calvinism is seen, first, in the fact that Whitefield and Wesley were accused of "enthusiasm" which was defined vaguely and abusively as any kind of religious excitement, and, second, in the fact that John Gill, in his *A Complete Body of Doctrinal and Practical Divinity*, said that spiritual joy "is not to be expressed by those who experience it; it is better experienced than expressed." Morden, *Offering Christ*, 20.

4. Quoted from John Ryland's biography in Morden, *Offering Christ*, 103.

5. Fuller, *Works*, 2:387 (see chap. 2, n. 7).

6. Morden, *Offering Christ*, 8.

(with Rom. 6:14), and he thought for a while that he had been saved. But the experience proved to be abortive.[7]

What Fuller came to see was that High Calvinism had shifted the meaning of faith from focusing on the objective person and promises of Christ onto the subjective state of our own hearts. In other words, saving faith became faith that I am experiencing the regenerating work of God—faith that I am elect. Or, as Fuller put it, the High Calvinists said that faith is to "believe the goodness of their state." To this he responded:

> If this be saving faith, it must inevitably follow that it is not the duty of unconverted sinners; for they are not interested in Christ [that is, they are not yet united to him], and it cannot possibly be their duty to believe a lie. But if it can be proved that the proper object of saving faith is not our being interested in Christ [that is, our being already united to him], but the glorious gospel of the ever blessed God, (which is true, whether we believe it or not,) a contrary inference must be drawn; for it is admitted, on all hands, that it is the duty of every man to believe what God reveals.[8]

In fact, Fuller goes on to show that

> nothing can be an object of faith, except what God has revealed in his word; but the interest that any individual has in Christ . . . is not revealed. . . . The Scriptures

---

7. Ibid., 28.
8. Fuller, *Works*, 2:333.

always represent faith as terminating on something [outside of] us; namely, on Christ, and the truths concerning him. . . . The person, blood, and righteousness of Christ *revealed in the Scriptures as the way of a sinner's acceptance with God*, are, properly speaking, the objects of our faith; for without such a revelation it were impossible to believe in them. . . . That for which he ought to have trusted in him was the obtaining of mercy, in case he applied for it. For this there was a complete warrant in the gospel declarations.[9]

In other words, we should not say to unbelievers, "Wait until you feel some warrant of faith so that you can trust in that." Rather, we should say: "Christ is the glorious, divine Son of God. His death and resurrection are sufficient to cover all your sins.[10] He promises to receive everyone who comes to him, and he promises to forgive all who trust in him. Therefore, come to him and trust him and you will be saved. If you wonder whether you are elect or whether you are regenerate, cease wondering and do what Christ has commanded you to do. Receive him, trust in him, cast

---

9. Ibid., 2:334, 340, 342, emphasis original.

10. On the extent of the atonement, Fuller found himself again defending the Scripture against High Calvinists and Arminians, who both thought that "particular redemption" made the free offer of the gospel to all illogical. His position is that the death of Christ is not to be conceived of "commercially" in the sense that it purchased effectually a limited number such that if more believed they could not be atoned for.

On the other hand, if the atonement of Christ proceed not on the principle of commercial, but of moral justice, or justice as it relates to *crime*—if its grand object were to express the divine displeasure against sin (Romans 8:3) and so to render the exercise of mercy, in all the ways wherein sovereign wisdom should determine to apply it, consistent with righteousness (Romans 3:25)—*if it be in itself equal to the salvation of the whole world, were the whole world to embrace it*—and if the peculiarity which attends it consists not in its insufficiency to save more than are saved, but in the sovereignty of its application—no such inconsistency can justly be ascribed to it. (ibid., 2:373–74, emphasis added)

yourself on him for his promised mercy. And you will prove to be elect and to be regenerate."

Fuller the Calvinist

Fuller is a Calvinist. He says, "The Scriptures clearly ascribe both repentance and faith wherever they exist to divine influence [e.g., Eph. 2:8; 2 Tim. 2:25–26]." He believes in irresistible grace. But what he is arguing against is that one has to know before he believes that he is being irresistibly called or regenerated.

> Whatever necessity there may be for a change of heart in order [for one to believe], it is neither necessary nor possible that the party should be conscious of it till he has believed. It is necessary that the eyes of a blind man should be opened before he can see; but it is neither necessary nor possible for him to know that his eyes are open till he does see.[11]

---

11. Ibid., 2:383. In other words, the limitation of the atonement lies not in the sufficiency of its worth to save all the sinners in the world, but in the design of God to apply that infinite sufficiency to those whom he chooses.

As the application of redemption is solely directed by sovereign wisdom, so, like every other event, it is the result of *previous design*. That which is actually done was *intended* to be done. Hence the salvation of those that are saved is described as the end which the Savior had in view: "He gave himself for us, that he might redeem us from all iniquity, and purify unto himself a peculiar people, zealous of good works." Herein, it is apprehended, consists the peculiarity of redemption.

There is no contradiction between this peculiarity of *design* in the death of Christ, and the universal obligation of those who hear the gospel to believe in him, or universal invitation being addressed to them. (ibid., 2:374, emphasis original)

In this position, as in so many, Fuller was in line with his decisive mentor, Jonathan Edwards, who wrote in *The Freedom of the Will*:

Christ in some sense might be said to die for all, and to redeem all visible Christians, yea, the whole world by his death; yet there must be something particular in the design of his death, with respect to such as he intended should actually be saved thereby. . . . God has the actual salvation of redemption of a certain number in his proper absolute design, and of a certain number only; and therefore such a design only can be prosecuted in anything God does, in order to the salvation of men.

Fuller steadfastly refuses to let ostensible Calvinistic or Arminian logic override what he sees in Scripture. And ironically, High Calvinism and Arminianism are here standing on the same pretended logic against Scripture. Both argue that it is absurd and cruel to require of any man what is beyond his power to perform. Or to put it the way Fuller does:

> They are agreed in making the grace of God necessary to the accountableness of sinners with regard to spiritual obedience. The one [High Calvinism] pleads for graceless sinners being free from obligation, the other [Arminianism] admits of obligation but founds it on the notion of universal grace. Both are agreed that where there is no grace there is no duty. But if grace be the ground of obligation, it is no more grace, but debt.[12]

"The whole weight of this objection," he says, "rests upon the supposition *that we do not stand in need of the Holy Spirit to enable us to comply with our duty.*"[13] In other words, both High Calvinists and Arminians rejected the prayer of St. Augustine, "Give me the grace to do as you command, and command me to do what you will."[14] But Fuller says, "To me it appears that the necessity of Divine influence, and even of a change of heart, prior to believing,

---

(Jonathan Edwards, *The Freedom of the Will*, ed. Paul Ramsey, vol. 1 of *The Works of Jonathan Edwards* [New Haven, CT: Yale University Press, 1985], 435)

12. Fuller, *Works*, 2:379.
13. Ibid., emphasis original.
14. Augustine, *Confessions* 10.29, trans. R. S. Pine-Coffin (New York: Penguin, 1961), 233.

is perfectly consistent with its being the immediate duty of the unregenerate."[15] Why? Because the Scripture shows it to be the case, and Jonathan Edwards provides categories that help make sense out of it. Concerning the biblical witness, Fuller writes:

> The same things are required in one place which are promised in another: "Only fear the Lord, and serve him in truth with all your heart."—"I will put my fear in their hearts that they shall not depart from me." When the sacred writers speak of the divine precepts, they neither disown them nor infer from them a self-sufficiency to conform to them, but turn them into prayer: "Thou hast commanded us to keep thy precepts diligently. Oh that my ways were directed to keep thy statutes!" In fine, the Scriptures uniformly teach us that all our sufficiency to do good or to abstain from evil is from above; repentance and faith, therefore, may be duties, notwithstanding their being the gifts of God.[16]

Natural Inability and Moral Inability

In his most famous work, *The Gospel Worthy of All Acceptation*, Fuller piles text upon text in which unbelievers are addressed with the duty to believe.[17] These are his

---

15. Fuller, *Works*, 2:381.
16. Ibid., 2:380. "If an upright heart toward God and man be not itself required of us, nothing is or can be required; for all duty is comprehended in the acting-out of the heart" (ibid., 2:382).
17. See ibid., 2:343–66, where most of these texts are explained. See, for example, Ps. 2:11–12; Isa. 55:1–7; Jer. 6:16; John 5:23; 6:29; 12:36. Fuller aligns himself, at this point, with John Owen, who wrote, "When the apostle beseecheth us to be 'reconciled' to God, I would know whether it be not a part of our duty to yield obedience? If not, the expectation is frivolous and vain" (quoted in Fuller, *Works*, 2:353).

final court of appeal against the High Calvinists, who use their professed logic to move from biblical premises to unbiblical conclusions. But he finds Edwards very helpful in answering the High Calvinist objection on another level. Remember, the objection is that "it is absurd and cruel to require of any man what is beyond his power to perform." In other words, a man's inability to believe removes his responsibility to believe (and our duty to command people to believe). In response to this objection, Fuller brings forward the distinction between moral inability and natural inability. This was the key insight which he learned from Jonathan Edwards, and he gives him credit for it on the third page of *The Gospel Worthy*.[18]

The distinction is this: *Natural inability* is owing to the lack of "rational faculties, bodily powers, or external advantages"; but *moral inability* is owing to the lack of inclination because of an averse will. Natural inability does in fact remove obligation. Fuller cites Romans 2:12 as a pointer to this truth: "For all who have sinned without the law will also perish without the law, and all who have sinned under the law will be judged by the law." In other words, there is a correlation between what you will be held accountable for and what you had natural access to.

But moral inability does not excuse. It does not remove

---

18. Referring to himself in the third person as the author, Fuller writes:

He had also read and considered, as well as he was able, President Edwards's *Inquiry into the Freedom the Will* . . . on the difference between natural and moral inability. He found much satisfaction in the distinction as it appeared to him to carry with it its own evidence—to be clearly and fully contained in the Scriptures. . . . The more he examined the Scriptures, the more he was convinced that all inability ascribed to man, with respect to believing, arises from the perversion of his heart. (ibid., 2:330)

obligation. And this is the kind of inability the Bible is speaking about when it says, "The natural person does not accept the things of the Spirit of God, for they are folly to him, and he is not able to understand them because they are spiritually discerned" (1 Cor. 2:14; cf. Rom. 8:8). Fuller writes:

> There is an essential difference between an ability which is independent of the inclination, and one that is owing to nothing else. It is just as impossible, no doubt, for any person to do that which he has no mind to do, as to perform that which surpasses his natural powers; and hence it is that the same terms are used in one case as in the other.[19]

In other words, it is just as impossible for you to choose to do what you have no inclination to do as it is to do what you have no physical ability to do. But the inability owing to physical hindrances excuses, while the inability owing to a rebellious will does not.[20] This kind of reasoning was not Fuller's main reason for rejecting High Calvinism and Arminianism. Scripture was. But Edwards's categories helped Fuller make more sense of what he saw there.

---

19. Ibid., 2:377.
20. "He that, from the constitution of his nature, is absolutely unable to understand, or believe, or love a certain kind of truth, must of necessity, be alike unable to shut his eyes against it, to disbelieve, to reject, or to hate it. But it is manifest that all men are capable of the latter; it must therefore follow that nothing but the depravity of their heart renders them incapable of the former" (ibid., 2:378).

The Practical Effect for Missions

The all-important conclusion from all this exegetical, doctrinal, theological labor and controversy was the enormously practical implication for evangelism and world missions:

> I believe it is the duty of every minister of Christ plainly and faithfully to preach the gospel to all who will hear it; and, as I believe the inability of men to [do] spiritual things to be wholly of the moral, and therefore of the criminal kind—and that it is their duty to love the Lord Jesus Christ, and trust in him for salvation, though they do not; I therefore believe free and solemn addresses, invitations, calls, and warnings to them, to be not only consistent, but directly adapted as means, in the hand of the Spirit of God, to bring them to Christ. I consider it as part of my duty that I could not omit without being guilty of the blood of souls.[21]

Fuller's engagement at this level of intellectual rigor, as a pastor and a family man, may seem misplaced. The price was high in his church and in his family. But the fruit for the world was incalculably great. No one else was on the horizon to strike a blow against the church-destroying, evangelism-hindering, missions-killing doctrine of High Calvinism. Fuller did it, and the theological platform was laid for the launching of the greatest missionary movement in the world.

---

21. Morden, *Offering Christ*, 106.

Chapter Five

Fuller against Sandemanianism

In this chapter, I want to deal briefly with Fuller's engagement with Sandemanianism, then, in chapter 6, draw out some lessons for ourselves. Fuller's response to this deadening movement of his day was part of the platform for the missionary movement, and it is amazingly relevant for our day because of its bearing on the debates about the nature of justifying faith. Recently I tuned into an online debate between two Reformed thinkers, and there were elements of it that relate directly to Fuller's response to Sandemanianism (though no one there would be in the category of a Sandemanian). And again Fuller gets one of his decisive insights in this debate from Jonathan Edwards.

What Is Sandemanianism?

Robert Sandeman (1718–1771) spread the teaching that justifying faith is the mind's passive persuasion that the gospel statements are true. Here is the way Andrew Fuller summarizes this Sandemanianism: The distinguishing marks of the system relate

> to *the nature of justifying faith*. This Mr. S. [Sande-man] constantly represents as the bare belief of the bare truth; by which definition he intends, as it would seem, to exclude from it everything pertaining to the will and the affections, except as effects produced by it. . . . "Everyone," says he, "who obtains a just *notion* of the person and work of Christ, or whose *notion* corresponds to what is testified of him, is justified, and finds peace with God simply by that notion."
>
> This notion he considers as the effect of truth being impressed upon the mind, and denies that the mind is active in it. "He who maintains," says he, "that we are justified only by faith, and at the same time affirms . . . that faith is a work exerted by the human mind, undoubtedly maintains, if he had any meaning to his words, that we are justified by a work exerted by the human mind."[1]

Sandeman's aim is to protect the doctrine of justification by faith alone. He believes that if faith has any movement of mind or will or affections toward God, it is an act and therefore a work and would therefore compromise the doctrine. To protect the doctrine, he denies that faith has any activity in it at all. Implicit is that faith is not a virtue. It

---

1. Fuller, *Works*, 2:566–67, emphasis original (see chap. 2, n. 7). Sandeman took his view so seriously that he saw the mainstream Puritan writers (including men like Flavel, Boston, Guthrie, and the Erskines) as furnishing "a devout path to hell" (Sandeman quoted in ibid., 2:566).

does not partake of any goodness or newness in the soul. He therefore does not see regeneration as preceding and enabling faith, for that would make faith an acting of the renewed heart, and therefore we would be justified by the goodness of what we do. So faith must be defined as perfectly consistent with a soul that is in actual enmity with God, before there is any renewal at all.

Sandeman's main support for this view is the meaning of the term *ungodly* in Romans 4:5, "To the one who does not work but believes in him who justifies the ungodly, his faith is counted as righteousness." He argues that this term must mean that there is no godly or virtuous or renewed or active quality about our faith, for if there were, we would not be called "ungodly." So he defines faith as a passive persuasion of the truth in which the mind is not active. So faith can coexist with ungodliness, understood as the total absence of any renewal or godly act of the soul.[2]

For the Sake of the Church and the Nations

Fuller found this both unbiblical and deadening to the churches. To sever the roots of faith in regeneration, and to strip faith of its holiness, and to deny its active impulse to produce the fruit of love (Gal. 5:6) was to turn the church into an intellectualistic gathering of passive people who are afraid of their emotions and who lack any passion for worship or missions.[3] Therefore, Fuller, the lover of God and

---

2. See how Fuller explains this argument of Sandeman in ibid., 2:568.
3. "Their intellectualized view of faith probably accounted for what Fuller and Sutcliff saw as the arid nature of many of their churches. . . . Most centrally, they were not suffi-

missions, waged another battle against Sandemanianism for the sake of the church and the nations.

Fuller offers a hundred pages of small-print argument in twelve letters compiled under the title *Strictures on Sandemanianism*.[4] He points out, for example, that faith is a kind of "work" or act of the soul because Jesus says so in John 6:28–29: "Then they said to him, 'What must we do, to be doing the works of God?' Jesus answered them, 'This is the work of God, that you believe in him whom he has sent.'"[5] Fuller also observes that it is the uniform witness of Scripture that "without repentance there is no forgiveness."[6] He also shows that the meaning of faith in the New Testament is revealed with many parallel expressions that imply the good action of the heart (for example, *to receive Christ*, John 1:12; or *to come to Christ*, John 6:35).

---

ciently committed to the spread of the gospel" (Peter Morden, *Offering Christ to the World: Andrew Fuller (1754–1815) and the Revival of Eighteenth Century Particular Baptist Life*, Studies in Baptist History and Thought 8 [Carlisle: Paternoster, 2003], 150).

4. Fuller, *Works*, 2:561–646. Here are two sample arguments for not taking "ungodly" in Rom. 4:5 to mean that faith in the justified believer has no character of holiness:

[Argument #1:] Neither Abraham nor David, whose cases the apostle selects for the illustration of his argument, was, at the time referred to, the enemy of God. . . . But the truth is, [Abraham] had been a believer in God and a true worshiper of him for many years, at the time when he is said to have believed in God, and it was counted to him for righteousness, Genesis 12:1–3; 15:6; Hebrews 11:8. Here then is an account of one who had walked with God for a series of years "working not, but believing on him that justifieth the ungodly;" a clear proof that by "working not" the apostle did not mean a wicked inaction, but a renunciation of works as the ground of acceptance with God. (ibid., 3:717)

[Argument #2:] It has been said that the term ungodly is never used but to describe the party as being under actual enmity of God at the time. I apprehend this is a mistake. Christ is said to have died for the "ungodly." Did he then lay down his life only for those who, at the time, were actually his enemies? If so, he did not die for any of the Old Testament saints, nor for any of the godly who were then alive, nor even for his own apostles. All that can in truth be said is, that, whatever were the characters at the time, he died for them as ungodly; and thus it is that he "justifieth the ungodly." (ibid., 2:404)

5. Ibid., 3:718. But he adds immediately, as we will see below, "But that we are justified by it as a work, or as a part of moral obedience . . . I utterly deny."

6. Ibid., 3:716.

STRICTURES

ON

SANDEMANIANISM,

IN

TWELVE LETTERS TO A FRIEND.

BY ANDREW FULLER.

NOTTINGHAM:
PRINTED BY C. SUTTON;

AND SOLD BY BUTTON, 24, AND BURDITT, 60, PATERNOSTER
ROW; WILLIAMS AND SMITH, STATIONERS' COURT; GAR-
DINER, 20, PRINCES STREET, OXFORD STREET, LONDON;
OLIPHANT AND BALFOUR, EDINBURGH; AND J. AND A.
DUNCAN, GLASGOW.

1810.

PRICE THREE SHILLINGS AND SIXPENCE.

Title page of the first edition of Fuller's
Strictures on Sandemanianism

So Fuller denies that faith is a mere passive persuasion of the mind, but asserts that it is the holy fruit of regeneration which has in it the good impulse to be "working through love" (Gal. 5:6).[7] To see this is vital for the life of the church and the power of world missions. How then does he reconcile this with Romans 4:5, which says that God "justifies the ungodly"? Here is Fuller's answer:

---

7. "Unbelief [is not] the same thing as unholiness, enmity, or disobedience; but it is not so distinct from either as not to partake of the same general nature. It is not only the root of all other sin, but is itself a sin. In like manner, faith is not only the root of all other obedience, but is itself an exercise of obedience. It is called 'obeying the truth,' and 'obeying the gospel'" (ibid., 2:575).

> This term [*ungodly* in Rom. 4:5], I apprehend, is not designed, in the passage under consideration, to express the actual *state of mind* which the party at the time possesses, but the *character* under which God considers him in bestowing the blessing of justification upon him. Whatever be the present state of the sinner's mind— whether he be a haughty Pharisee or a humble publican—*if he possess nothing which can in any degree balance the curse which stands against him, or at all operate as a ground of acceptance with God, he must be justified, if at all, as unworthy, ungodly, and wholly out of regard to the righteousness of the mediator.*[8]

Fuller uses the analogy of a magnet to help us see that faith can have qualities about it that are not in view when God counts faith as justifying:

> Whatever holiness there is in [faith], it is not this, but the obedience of Christ, that constitutes our justifying righteousness. Whatever other properties the magnet may possess, it is as pointing invariably to the north that it guides the mariner; and whatever other properties faith may possess, it is as receiving Christ, and bringing us into union with him, that it justifies.[9]

8. Ibid., 3:715, emphasis added to the latter sentence, otherwise original.
9. Ibid., 1:281.

By believing in Jesus Christ the sinner becomes vitally united to him, or, as the Scriptures express it, "joined to the Lord," and is of "one spirit with him"; and this union, according to the divine constitution, as revealed in the gospel, is the ground of an interest in his righteousness. Agreeable to this is the following language: "There is now, therefore *no condemnation* to them that are *in* Christ Jesus."—"Of him are ye *in* Christ Jesus, who of God is made unto us *righteousness*," etc.—"That I may be found *in* him not having mine own righteousness which is of the law, but that which is through faith in Christ." (ibid., 2:384, emphasis original)

The Uniqueness of Faith

Fuller points out that faith is unique among all the other graces that grow in the renewed heart. It is a *"peculiarly receiving grace."*

> Thus it is that justification is ascribed to faith, because it is by faith that we receive Christ; and thus it is by *faith only*, and not by any other grace. Faith is peculiarly a *receiving grace* which none other is. Were we said to be justified by repentance, by love, or by any other grace, it would convey to us the idea of something good in us being the *consideration* on which the blessing was bestowed; but justification by faith conveys no such idea. On the contrary, it leads the mind directly to Christ, in the same manner as saying of a person that he lives by *begging* leads to the idea of his living on *what he freely receives.*"[10]

What matters, Fuller says, concerning the meaning of the justification of the ungodly is not that we possess no holy affections in the moment of justification by faith, "but that, whatever we possess we make *nothing* of it as a ground of acceptance, 'counting all things but loss and dung that we may win and be found in him.'"[11] Faith is a duty. It is an act of the soul. It is a good effect of regeneration. "Yet," Fuller

---

10. Ibid., 1:281, emphasis original. "By faith we receive the benefit; but the benefit arises not from faith, but from Christ. Hence the same thing which is described in some places to faith, is in others ascribed to the obedience, death, and resurrection of Christ" (ibid., 1:282).
11. Ibid., 2:406, emphasis original.

says, "it is not as such, but as uniting us to Christ and deriving righteousness from him, that it justifies."[12]

Faith: A Holy Act That Justifies the Ungodly

Fuller concludes his book *The Gospel Worthy of All Acceptation* with reference back to the New Testament preachers:

> The ground on which they took their stand was "Cursed is everyone who continueth not in all things written in the book of the law to do them" [Gal. 3:10]. Hence they inferred the impossibility of the sinner being justified in any other way than for the sake of him who was "made a curse for us;" and hence it clearly follows, that whatever holiness any sinner may possess before, in, or after believing, it is of no account whatever as a ground of acceptance with God.[13]

Which means that God justifies us under the consideration of our unworthiness, our ungodliness, because of Christ, not under the consideration of any holiness in us. In this way, Fuller is able to retain the crucial biblical meaning of faith as a holy acting of the will flowing from regeneration, and yet say with Paul, "To the one who does not work but believes in him who *justifies the ungodly*, his faith is counted as righteousness" (Rom. 4:5).

---

12. Ibid., 2:572. At this point, Fuller refers to Jonathan Edwards and gives him credit for this insight.
13. Ibid., 2:392–93.

One Great Enemy: Global Unbelief

The sum of the matter is that Fuller had one great enemy he wanted to defeat—global unbelief in Jesus Christ. He believed that the kingdom of Christ would triumph, and he meant to be an instrument in the conquering of unbelief in India and to the ends of the earth. Standing in the way of that triumph in his generation were false views of justifying faith and false views of gospel preaching. Sandemanianism had ripped the life and power out of faith so that it was powerless in worship and missions. Hyper-Calvinism had muzzled the gospel cry of "the Bride" ("The Spirit and the Bride say, 'Come.' And let the one who hears say, 'Come.' And let the one who is thirsty come; let the one who desires take the water of life without price," Rev. 22:17). For the sake of the life of the church and the salvation of the nations, Fuller took up the battle for truth.

Chapter Six

The Vital Link
between Doctrine and
World Missions

What shall we learn from this? We should learn the vital link between the doctrinal faithfulness of the church and the cause of world missions. The main impulse of our day is in the other direction. Everywhere you turn there is pressure to believe that missions depends on not disputing about doctrine. As soon as you engage another professing Christian in controversy over some biblical issue, the cry will go up, "Stop wasting your time and be about missions." What we learn from Fuller is that those cries are, at best, historically naïve and, at worst, a smoke screen for the uninhibited spread of error.

One crucial lesson from Andrew Fuller's life is that the exegetical and doctrinal defense of true justifying faith and true gospel preaching in the end did not hinder but advanced the greatest missionary movement in world history. Getting Christian experience biblically right and getting the gospel biblically right are essential for the power and perseverance and fruitfulness of world missions.

Wrong Inferences Produce Deadly Mistakes

We should learn from Fuller's conflicts that deadly mistakes come from drawing wrong inferences from texts based on superficial claims of logic: If God justifies the ungodly, then faith must be ungodly because God justifies by faith. If the natural man cannot receive the message of the cross, then don't urge him to receive it; it's pointless and cruel. Sound logic is not the enemy of exegesis. But more errors than we know flow from the claim to logic that contradicts the Bible:

- If God is love, there cannot be predestination.
- If Stephen says Israel has resisted God, then God cannot overcome our rebellion irresistibly.
- If men are accountable for their choices, they must be ultimately self-determining.
- If God is good, innocent people cannot suffer so much.
- If God rules all things including sin, he must be a sinner.
- If God rules all things, there is no point in praying.
- If God threatens a person with not entering the kingdom, he or she cannot have eternal security.
- If Christ died for all, he cannot have purchased anything particular for the elect.

Fuller shows us that the best antidote against the wrong use of logic is not, first, better logic but better knowledge of the Bible, which is the best warning system for when logic is being misused.

Global Impact for the Glory of Christ

There is a kind of inner logic to Fuller's life and battles and global fruitfulness. His engagement with Sandemanianism highlights the importance of vital, authentic spiritual experience over against sterile, intellectualistic faith. His engagement with hyper-Calvinism highlights the importance of objective gospel truth. These two things set the stage for assaulting global unbelief. Authentic subjective experience of God plus authentic objective truth of God leads to authentic practical mission for God. Holy faith plus worthy gospel yields world vision.

Therefore, devote yourself to experiencing Christ in the gospel biblically and authentically. And devote yourself to understanding Christ in the gospel biblically and authentically. And may God ignite that experience and that understanding in such a way that your life will count like Andrew Fuller's for the cause of world evangelization to the glory of Christ.

❄ desiringGod

Everyone wants to be happy. Our website was born and built for happiness. We want people everywhere to understand and embrace the truth that *God is most glorified in us when we are most satisfied in him.* We've collected more than thirty years of John Piper's speaking and writing, including translations into more than forty languages. We also provide a daily stream of new written, audio, and video resources to help you find truth, purpose, and satisfaction that never end. And it's all available free of charge, thanks to the generosity of people who've been blessed by the ministry.

If you want more resources for true happiness, or if you want to learn more about our work at Desiring God, we invite you to visit us at www.desiringGod.org.

www.desiringGod.org

Also Available from
John Piper

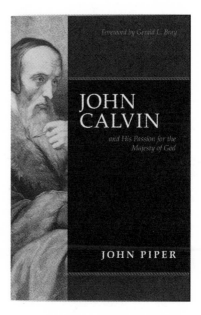